I
AM
WORTHY
ENOUGH
for
MARRIAGE

30 Prayers to Prepare me to Become a
Wife

I
AM
WORTHY
ENOUGH
for
MARRIAGE

30 Prayers to Prepare me to Become a Wife

YOLANDA MARSHALL NICKERSON

Glimpse of Glory
CHRISTIAN BOOK PUBLISHING

Mr. & Mrs. Larry Nickerson
Married on May 3, 2014

This book is dedicated to all the single women who have been praying to God for a husband. I want to encourage each of you by letting you know that God has heard your prayer, and He will respond at the appointed time. I decree that by the Grace of God, your husband will find you and obtain Favor from the Lord.

CONTENTS

INTRODUCTION

Have you been praying about being married? Do you feel like He is taking too long to answer your prayer? Does it seem like God has not heard your prayer? Do you feel like you have been waiting forever? Are you losing hope for marriage? If God were to send you a husband in this season of your life, do you honestly feel like you are prepared for marriage?

Are you dealing with some stuff mentally from past relationships? Are you currently settling in a relationship or have you settled in a previous relationship? Do you believe that God showed you any signs of that being the wrong relationship for you, but you ignored what He showed you? Do you understand that when you settle for just any man in a relationship it can hinder you from receiving the man that God has set aside for you for marriage?

God sees and knows the desire of your heart for marriage, and He wants to fulfill that desire. But He just wants to prepare you to become a wife first. He wants to rid you of some things that could hinder your marriage from growing. He wants to heal you mentally and emotionally. He wants to restore your self-esteem and confidence that was damaged in previous relationships. He wants to teach you how not to settle for just any man. He wants to show you how worthy you are of having "the man" that He has for you. Trust me. God is going to send you the husband that He has for you at the appointed time He desires to establish a union between the two of you in the earth realm.

I want you to know that your marriage has already been established in Heaven. It was established before the foundation of the earth. I decree and declare that you will soon be a Mrs...

I AM WORTHY ENOUGH FOR MARRIAGE

PRAYER 1

RELATIONSHIP WITH GOD

Your relationship with God is the most important relationship that you will ever have. It is an awesome thing when you give your life to God, but it does not automatically mean that you have a relationship with Him.

You can develop and build a strong relationship with God by spending time with Him in prayer, and through reading and studying His Word, and also through daily meditation. When you consistently do those things—and you are encouraged to do them while you are single—your relationship with Him will grow stronger and stronger each and every day, and there will be nothing or no one who would be able to break up that relationship between you and God.

Now after you have established a relationship with God, it will be easier to develop and build a covenant with the husband that He has for you. It is a beautiful thing when two people who have a relationship with God are brought together in a sacred union. It is easier for both of them to put God at the helm of their union.

Let this be your prayer:

God, I pray that You prepare me to become a wife by teaching me how to build a strong, healthy relationship with You. By having a relationship with You, I trust that You will make sure that the union between my future husband and I will be in You and that it will have the capacity to grow stronger in You for the lifetime of our marriage. Amen.

I AM WORTHY ENOUGH FOR MARRIAGE

PRAYER 2

EMOTIONAL HEALING

It is so very important for you to be emotionally healed prior to marrying. If your emotions have been damaged from your current or previous relationship, then the negative effects of your emotions can easily spill over into your marriage. You certainly do not want that to happen. You want to make sure that when you enter into your marriage, you are a healed and a whole woman, not a broken woman with unhealed emotions.

Let this be your prayer:

God, I pray that You prepare me to become a wife by healing my emotions and making me whole. It is my sincere desire to be emotionally stable and healthy so that my actions, my feelings, and my thoughts towards the husband that You have for me will be pure, rich, and wholesome. Remove from my heart the hurt, the pain, the anger, and the disappointments that stemmed from the past relationship(s) that damaged my emotions. Amen.

PRAYER 3

MENTAL HEALING

It is critical that you are mentally healed prior to marrying, too. If you experienced negative behavior in your current or previous relationship, I am certain that it has affected you mentally. When someone does or says something to make one feel less than, that is considered negative behavior. Has your current or previous mate ever said harsh and disparaging words to you that deeply hurt you and made you feel bad about yourself?

19

You see, negative words spoken to a person does not just magically go away. Those words can linger on in the mind for days, weeks, months, and even years. Sometimes, you have to get counseling so that you can release those negative thoughts that stem from negative words that were spoken to you. More importantly, you have to ask God to heal your mind because you do not want negative thoughts lingering in your mind as you go into the ordained covenant He has for you.

Let this be your prayer:
God, I pray that You prepare me to become a wife by healing me mentally. Remove those negative thoughts from my mind that stem from negative words

that have been spoken to me. I pray that You allow me to get all of the help that I need through natural and spiritual counseling methods so that I can be mentally healthy for marriage. Amen.

PRAYER 4

COMPLETE IN YOUR SINGLENESS

You must learn how to embrace the season that you now find yourself in, without thinking that you need a man to complete you. You should focus on being complete in your singleness. Be intentional about enjoying yourself in this season. Travel. Have fun. Hang out with your friends. Go shopping. Go to a nice restaurant for breakfast, lunch, or dinner. Do the things that make your heart smile and that will also put a smile on your face.

23

Let this be your prayer:

God, I pray that You prepare me to become a wife by allowing me to be complete as a single woman. Teach me how to be happy and enjoy this season of it being just me. Give me the drive to do fun and memorable things while I maintain a wholesome lifestyle. Amen.

PRAYER 5

BALANCED LIFE

When you are single, you can go and do as you please. Some single women may have a few restrictions if they have small children. But, in your singleness, you do not have to worry about consulting a spouse on whether or not you should go to a particular place or do a certain thing.

However, when you get married, things are a little different. A marriage is a unit and it requires that a husband and wife spend quality time with each and also put each other before anyone else, that includes family members, friends, and others. With that being said, you will not be able to just do as you please without consulting your spouse; that is why it is necessary that you learn how to have balance as a single woman. Learn how to say no to some things. You must also realize that you don't always have to be a part of everything that someone else is doing.

Let this be your prayer:

God, I pray that You prepare me to become a wife by helping me to have a balanced life. Teach me how to pull away from people, places, and things when needed, and help me to rest in You. Amen.

PRAYER 6

SELF-LOVE

It is impossible to effectively love someone else when you don't fully love yourself. Self-love needs to be exhibited in your life before you get married. You need to show yourself love by being kind to yourself, by embracing your imperfections, and by healing from your past hurts, pains, and disappointments. When you heal prior to marrying, it can prevent you from inflicting hurt and pain on the husband that God has for you. You will be able to love your husband in every way he will need to be loved.

Let this be your prayer:

God, I know that You are the source of love. I pray that You prepare me to become a wife by teaching me how to love myself, even beyond my flaws, so that I will be able to love the man that you will send to me that I will someday call my husband. I ask that You remove anything that could possibly hinder me from loving him throughout our marriage. Amen.

PRAYER 7

SELF-WORTH

According to Proverbs 31:10, your worth is far above rubies. Did you know that? It is very important to know your worth. When you know your worth, you will not accept less than God's best in any area of your life.

Now it is quite easy to settle for an unhealthy and abusive relationship (or anything else) when you don't know your worth. It is not uncommon for your value to be diminished when you are in that kind of relationship.

29

You can easily experience name calling, cheating, and other negative actions when you are in a relationship with a man who does not value your worth. You will need to steer away from relationships like that in order to embrace the one that God has for you.

Let this be your prayer:

God, I pray that You prepare me to become a wife by showing me how to value my worth. Don't let me or anyone else diminish my value. Keep Your arms around me and shield me from being emotionally drawn to just any man and settle in a relationship that is not intended for me. As of this moment, I desire to be found by the man that You have for me, one who

30

will appreciate and value my worth.
Amen.

PRAYER 8

SELF-ESTEEM

So many things can happen in your life to pull down your self-esteem. It is not uncommon for your self-esteem to be destroyed when you encounter certain situations in your life. Some childhood scars can create self-esteem issues. How much more would a bad relationship do to your self-esteem. I remember being in a relationship that not only nearly sucked the life out of me, but it nearly destroyed my self-esteem. My self-esteem was not only unhealthy for months, but years. This may very well be your truth, too. You will certainly need to get your self-esteem intact while you are single. I am a living witness that God will and can help you with your self-esteem.

Let this be your prayer:

God, I pray that You prepare me to become a wife by making my self-esteem healthy again. Help me to feel good about myself. Amen.

PRAYER 9

SELF-ACCEPTANCE

You must learn to accept every part of yourself before you can even think about accepting the man that God has for you. You have imperfections that you must learn to accept. You have flaws that you must learn to accept. You have good qualities and you have bad qualities that you must learn to accept.

You are not a perfect person. But you can and should always strive to become the best version of yourself, while still loving yourself, being kind

35

to yourself, and accepting yourself where you are right now.

Let this be your prayer:

God, I pray that You prepare me to become a wife by helping me to accept myself right where I am. Help me not to focus on the mistakes that I have made, and don't let me reject myself or beat myself up over those mistakes. I know that I am not perfect, Lord, and I have flaws, but I ask that You help me become a better version of myself as I desire to be more and more like You every day. Amen.

PRAYER **10**

SELF-CARE

Self-care is very important, and it is necessary. If you have been putting yourself on the backburner, you need to stop it *now*. You must start taking care of yourself today. You cannot afford to neglect yourself emotionally, mentally, spiritually, or physically.

There is no way you can effectively care or do for a husband and give him the "best part" of you when you are broken, drained, and empty. I once heard someone say, "You cannot pour from an empty cup." I totally agree with that statement.

It would be beneficial for you to get yourself together before you get married so that you will be able to pour into your husband from a full cup, a full place, lacking nothing.

Let this be your prayer:

God, I pray that You prepare me to become a wife by helping me to take care of myself. I do not desire to be selfish, but I do desire to be healthy and strong enough to do what You have called me to do, and to also serve effectively in my role as a wife whenever you decide to bless me with a husband. I believe that if I manage self-care, it would be easy to care for and pour into my husband. I know that I cannot pour from an empty cup, so I pray that You "fill my cup." I have no desire to be an empty wife. Amen.

I AM WORTHY ENOUGH FOR MARRIAGE

PRAYER 11

SELF-CONTROL

It is very important that you learn how to have self-control while you are single. If anger is rooted in your heart, you are encouraged to release it *now,* because it can be difficult for you to have a single measure of self-control in any given situation. It would be easier to walk into an argument than to walk away from an argument.

You have to make up in your mind that you are not going to let anything or anyone upset you to the point of losing control in a situation or getting out of character.

If you struggle with having self-control, this would be a good time to work on yourself and practice having self-control. Don't wait until you get married to do it. Do it *now* so that you will not go into a marriage being an angry and contentious woman who lacks self-control. A good scripture to read and meditate on is Proverbs 21:9, and it reads, "It is better to dwell in a corner of the housetop, than to share a house with a contentious woman."

Let this be your prayer:
God, I pray that You prepare me to become a wife by removing any anger that may be in my heart and teach me

how to have self-control. Help me to stay in full control when I encounter situations that are designed to make me get out of character. Help me to understand that every situation does not need a response from me. I desire to enter into the marriage that you have ordained for me, fully executing the fruit of the Spirit, according to Galatians 5:22-23. Amen.

PRAYER 12

INNER PEACE

Your mind and your heart can be filled with so much baggage from past relationships, and it just comes to a point where both of them need to be decluttered. When your mind and heart are free from baggage, you can experience that inner peace that you have probably been longing for. Seek the peace of God so that when you get married, you won't carry unnecessary baggage with you into your marriage.

Let this be your prayer:

God, I pray that You prepare me to become a wife by giving me inner peace. Declutter my mind and my heart *now.* Give me that "peace that surpasses all understanding," just as You said You would do in Your Word (Philippians 4:7). Amen.

PRAYER 13

HAPPINESS

When you are happily single, you will not be so quick to accept any type of man in your life. However, when you are not happy with yourself and feel you desperately need someone to complete you and make you happy, you can easily attract the wrong type of men.

Perhaps, you may have experienced a time when you were not happy with yourself and you thought that being in a relationship would make you happy, but you ended up in a relationship that

47

only made you miserable and sad. Don't feel bad. You are not alone. I have been there before, more than once. I settled in several relationships, and two failed marriages. I had to learn how to be happy with myself and live a happy single life before God sent me the man who He had for me, the husband who I have now been married to for over six years.

It is important that you also learn how to be happy with yourself while you are single, get to know yourself better and set healthy boundaries so that your next relationship will be with the man that God has for you.

Let this be your prayer:

God, I know that You are the source of my happiness, so I pray that You prepare me to become a wife by restoring my happiness and allowing me to experience the fullness of it in my singleness. I want to be able to add to my future husband's happiness and have a happy home when you send him to me. Amen.

I AM WORTHY ENOUGH FOR MARRIAGE

PRAYER **14**

FORGIVENESS

Forgiveness is necessary, and it can also be rewarding. In order to move forward in life and receive unlimited blessings from God, you must forgive.

You must first forgive yourself, and then anyone who has wronged you, that includes forgiving the man who hurt you in your current or in a previous relationship.

You certainly do not want to enter a marriage with a bitter, angry, stony and unforgiving heart. You should desire to have a merry heart because it does good like medicine, according to Proverbs Chapter 17, verse 22. When you have a merry heart, forgiveness cannot lie dormant in your heart. In order to keep a merry heart, you have to forgive quickly.

Let this be your prayer:

God, I pray that You prepare me to become a wife by helping me to forgive myself first, and then anyone else that I may have not forgiven. I don't ever want to be hindered from receiving anything from You because of being an unforgiving person. I desire to live a life of forgiveness, and I know that I can do this with Your help. Amen.

PRAYER 15

WISDOM

It is a great spiritual benefit to have wisdom and to know how to use it to make sound decisions daily. Wisdom is also a spiritual gift (1 Corinthians, Chapter 12, verse 8). It defeats the purpose of having wisdom if you are not going to use it, or you simply do not know how to use it.

If you feel that you don't have wisdom or don't know how to use it, don't beat yourself up. Now is the time to ask God for help. Ask Him to not let you make another move or a decision without applying wisdom to that decision. When wisdom is not applied, it is not uncommon for one to make emotional decisions in every area of their life. You certainly don't want that to happen again. You want to be able to make better decisions for the remainder of your single life and also when you become a wife.

Let this be your prayer:

God, I pray that You prepare me to become a wife by giving me wisdom. I desire to have wisdom so that I can make the best decisions as a single woman and when I get married, too. Amen.

PRAYER 16

INTERCESSORY PRAYER

The Bible tells us to pray without ceasing, according to 1 Thessalonians 5:17. If you do not have a consistent prayer life, you certainly need one. You should pray daily. Now is the perfect time to start praying about everything that concerns you.

You don't have to wait until you get married to start praying. You can start *now*. And when you get married, you will find it easier to grab your husband's hand and pray with him, and you will even intercede for him and on his behalf when needed. You will see just how powerful it is when you and your husband pray together, and also how God will grant your prayer requests, according to Matthew 18:19.

Let this be your prayer:

God, I pray that You prepare me to become a wife by giving me a praying spirit. I understand that it is important to pray about everything, and I desire to pray about everything while I am single so that when I get married, I will be accustomed to praying without ceasing. Amen.

PRAYER 17

RESPECT

Respecting yourself should not be something that you are made to do. It should be something that you desire to do, from dressing appropriately to having wholesome conversations to everything in between. When you respect yourself, you are sending a clear message to others that you not only deserve respect, but you also will not tolerate being disrespected on any level.

You have to set this standard while you are single, and if you feel that you need to do a little work in this area of your life, then you are encouraged to do it now. When your husband finds you, let him find a wholesome, classy woman who knows how to fully carry herself in a respectful manner.

Let this be your prayer:

God, I pray that You prepare me to become a wife by helping me to always respect myself. I desire to be found by my covenant partner in a respectful posture. Amen.

PRAYER 18

SUPPORT

You may be living out your dreams or you aspire to do a particular thing, and I am certain that the support from family members, friends and others mean a lot to you.

On the other hand, it can mean a lot to others when you gladly reciprocate that support. If you struggle with supporting others, you are encouraged to learn how to support others now; therefore, it will be much easier for you to support your husband when you get married. He will have dreams, aspirations, and goals, too, and he will need your continued prayers, love, and support. He should be able to feel the empowerment and spiritual push from a wife who understands what it means to give her full support to him.

Let this be your prayer:

God, I pray that You prepare me to become a wife by helping me to be a supportive person. I desire to fully support my future husband's dreams, aspiration, and goals when You bless me with him. Amen.

PRAYER **19**

SERVANTHOOD

According to Matthew 23:11, the greatest among you shall be your servant. In order to be good at serving others, you must first have a heart to serve. It would be difficult to serve anyone in your singleness, and even your husband when you get married, if you don't have the heart to do it. When your heart is far from serving, you will serve with an attitude and from a place of frustration, and that is not good at all.

Before you get married, you must realize that a marriage requires that both the wife and the husband serve each other, not with an attitude, not from a place of frustration, nor with any complaints. Just know that God wants your marriage to glorify Him. It makes Him proud when a husband and wife treat each other right.

Let this be your prayer:
God, I pray that You prepare me to become a wife by giving me the heart, the mindset, and the will to serve. I desire to serve the man you will bless me to marry. Amen.

PRAYER 20

TRUST

It is not uncommon to have trust issues if someone violates your trust. If you have encountered certain things (cheating, lying, etc.) in your current or previous relationship, this would be the kind of behavior that would lead to one having trust issues and it makes it so much more difficult to trust that person again, or even other people.

Learning how to trust again will be something that you will need God to help you with, and He will do that as you go through your emotional and mental healing process.

God wants to make sure you don't go into a marriage with trust issues. Having trust issues can be detrimental to your marriage, and you certainly do not want that to happen. You don't want to inflict harm on your husband because of your inability to trust due to past experiences.

Let this be your prayer:

God, I pray that You prepare me to become a wife by helping me to trust again. I don't want to have any trust issues when I get married. I ask that You remove from my mind all of the past experiences that have caused me to have trust issues. Amen.

PRAYER 21

GIVING

Giving is a part of God. It honors Him when you give. And giving is not just limited to money. You can also generously give in other areas, too.

If you are currently struggling with giving, you need to honestly make a conscious effort to be and do better in that area, and do it before marriage, because a marriage is about both giving and receiving. A marriage is not a one-sided union and it never will be when you have two unselfish people together.

You will need to make sure you give to your husband just as you would expect for him to give to you. You will need to give him your undivided attention when he needs to express himself. You will need to give him advice when he is faced with certain challenges. You will need to give him encouragement whenever he is feeling low. You will need to give him money when and if he needs it. You will even need to give him your body when he desires intimacy.

Let this be your prayer:
God, I pray that You prepare me to become a wife by helping me to give generously. I don't want to only be on the receiving end in my marriage. I

desire to be a compassionate helpmate who will be honored to give to my future husband whenever he needs anything. Amen.

PRAYER 22

FINANCIAL STABILITY

I am certain that you desire to marry a man who is financially stable, but you should desire to be financially stable, too. Allow me to share this again: a marriage is not a one-sided union. So, before you get married, it would be wise to have your finances in order.

If there is anything that you can do without, then make sure you eliminate it. Unnecessary spending can lead to financial problems and debt that can linger on for years. Be sure to set a budget and start saving, if you haven't already done so. Make sure that you are a good steward over your money.

If by any chance you struggle with managing money, you are strongly encouraged to seek a financial advisor and sign up for a personal financial planning class.

Let this be your prayer:

God, I pray that You prepare me to become a wife by helping me to bring my finances into proper alignment. I desire to be financially stable before I get married. I have no desire to enter into a marriage with a zero balance in my checking or my savings account. Amen.

PRAYER 23

COMMITMENT

Marriage is a big commitment that requires two people to be committed. Before you even make that kind of commitment, you will need to make sure that you follow through with other commitments you have already made and those that you will make. It is certainly not okay for you to commit to doing something and not follow through with it, unless there is an emergency that would prevent you from doing so.

There is success, joy, peace, and an overall good feeling on the other side of a commitment that you faithfully follow through with. When you are able to keep commitments that means your word will not be null and void. It actually means something, and it will make a difference in the lives you give your commitment to.

Let this be your prayer:

God, I pray that You prepare me to become a wife by helping me to follow through with any commitments that I make. I desire to honor my word when I give it to someone, and not default on it. I desire to be fully committed to the covenant partner that you have for me just as much as I desire for him to be committed to me. Amen.

I AM WORTHY ENOUGH FOR MARRIAGE

PRAYER 24

COMPASSIONATE

To be shown compassion is such an awesome feeling. When you show compassion, you can literally make a difference in someone's life. You can turn their frown into a smile. You can make them feel happy when they are feeling sad. You can brighten up their day when it appears to be dark and gloomy.

You should make every effort to show others compassion as often as you can. You can make a commitment right now to do it, and when you get married, you will find that it would be much easier to treat your husband with compassion.

Let this be your prayer:

God, I pray that You prepare me to become a wife by helping me to be more compassionate. Let me not only show compassion to myself, but to others as well. I desire to show my future husband compassion in every way possible when that appointed time comes. Amen.

PRAYER 25

COMMUNICATION

Communication is a very important factor in a marriage and it is needed in order for a marriage to fully thrive. So, while you are single, you should reflect upon how you respond to any given situation. Determine how you currently respond to those who may say something to offend you. When you use the wrong words to respond, it can stir up an argument and result in a negative outcome, but when the right words are used to respond, it can easily create peace and result in a positive outcome.

If you feel that you need to enhance your communication skills, now is the time to do it because when you get married, you and your husband will have those times when you all will disagree, and you need to know how to respond wisely. Always remember to watch the words you use and the tone of your voice.

Let this be your prayer:

God, I pray that You prepare me to become a wife by helping me to communicate my thoughts, concerns, and even my frustrations in a calm manner. Guide my tongue daily. Help me not to say the wrong thing that will cause harm to anyone. I desire to enter into the marriage that You have for me not only with the ability to effectively communicate my thoughts, and concerns, but I also want to be sensitive enough to listen to my husband when he has something on his mind and heart that he desires to share with me. Amen.

PRAYER 26

CONFLICT RESOLUTION

If there is ever a dispute between you and someone else, there is a need to respond calmly and peacefully. When you do not respond in this manner, situations can turn hostile and escalate into something that could easily have an adverse effect. You don't want that to happen.

If you currently do not know how to resolve problems without yelling, fussing, nagging, and getting in your feelings, you will not magically be able to resolve problems when you get married. As stated before, when you get married, there will be times when you and your husband will have disagreements, so it is very necessary for you to learn how to resolve conflict while you are single.

Here are a few conflict resolution skills that you should make note of: You should always practice listening to a person when they are sharing their thoughts and don't cut them off amid their sentence. You should never be so quick to get on the defense and respond negatively to any situation. You should always strive to maintain a calm tone and posture.

Let this be your prayer:

Heavenly Father, I pray that You prepare me for marriage by teaching me how to resolve matters peacefully. Don't let me be quick to jump to a conclusion regarding any situation as a single woman and even when I am married. Amen.

I AM WORTHY ENOUGH FOR MARRIAGE

PRAYER 27

SUBMISSION

Perhaps you may have experienced a bad relationship or a marriage where you found yourself submitting to a man who was abusive, did not have a relationship with God and certainly had not submitted to Him, so the thought of submission has probably put a bad taste in your mouth because your experience with submission was being trampled and controlled.

I can assure you that submission in a marriage that is ordained by God is a beautiful thing. You are not put in a position to be trampled or controlled. You are put in a position by God to submit to your husband by yielding to him in a loving, kind, meek, gentle, respectful, peaceful, and humble way.

Let this be your prayer:
Heavenly Father, I pray that You prepare me for marriage by teaching me how to submit, first to You. I desire to have full knowledge of submission, according to Your will and Your Word so that when I get married, it will be easy for me to submit to my husband. Amen.

PRAYER 28

AGREEMENT

When you are used to walking in the direction of your choice and doing things your way for so long as a single woman, it can be very difficult to walk in agreement with someone else, but walking in agreement is required in any marriage, and it is also necessary for a marriage to survive. The Bible asks the question in Amos 3:3 NLT translation, "Can two people walk together without agreeing on the direction?"

You can start preparing to walk in agreement with the man that God has for you. I can assure you that when you walk in agreement and be on one accord with your husband, you will experience unlimited blessings from God in your marriage.

Let this be your prayer:
Heavenly Father, I pray that You prepare me for marriage by giving me the mindset, the will, and the power to walk in agreement and to be on one accord with the husband that you have for me. Amen.

PRAYER 29

UNSELFISH DEVOTION

While it is important for you to put yourself first—and it is certainly easier to do that when you are single—when you get married there will be times you will need to temporarily lay aside your needs while catering to the needs of your husband. Those times will include when he simply needs a massage after a long day's work and you are literally too tired to give it, when he experiences sickness, when he becomes overwhelmed by life's situations and circumstances, when he faces opposition on the job that he can't just quit because he has a family to provide for, and so much more that he has to encounter being the head of the household.

That is what unselfish devotion is really all about. It's about taking some time to put the needs of others before your own needs sometimes. Knowing that it is not all about you will help you put things in perspective.

Let this be your prayer:

Heavenly Father, I pray that You prepare me for marriage by helping me to be willing to lay aside my needs and put the husband that you have for me first when needed throughout our marriage. Remove any selfish motives and help me to realize it is never all about me. Amen.

PRAYER 30

PATIENCE

If you have a hard time being patient, you can easily find yourself getting ahead of God's timing and making wrong decisions. Everything that you desire for God to do in your life and/or you have prayed for Him to manifest, will not always happen quickly. You have to patiently wait for certain things to manifest in your life, and that includes getting married.

Now is a very good time to practice patience while you are single, because if you don't, when you get married, there will be certain times you may want your husband to make quick decisions based upon your emotions and inability to wait, when as the head of the household, he will need to wait for God to speak to Him and give Him instructions and the permission to do a certain thing for you and your family.

Your husband will know that God will hold him accountable for every decision that he will make for his family, so don't go into a marriage expecting him to be in a hurry about matters that he will need to seek God's approval for first. Again, be sure to practice being patient in your singleness.

Let this be your prayer:

Heavenly Father, I pray that You prepare me for marriage by helping me to practice patience. Don't let me get ahead of You anymore by moving too quick on matters that require me to wait on You. I will commit to wait patiently for you to send me the man of my dreams, the One that you have already ordained to be my husband. Fill my heart with excitement as I wait and give me the confidence and assurance that my husband will arrive in Your perfect timing. Amen.

I AM WORTHY ENOUGH FOR MARRIAGE

YOUR PERSONAL DECLARATION AND PRAYER REQUEST TO GOD ABOUT THE GODLY MAN YOU DESIRE

("Write the vision and make it plain")

_____

_____

_____

_____

_____

_____

_____

_____

_____

_____

_____

_____

_____

_____

_____

_____

_____

_____

_____

_____

_____

_____

_____

_____

_____

_____

_____

_____

_____

_____

_____

_____

_____

_____

_____

_____

_____

_____

_____

_____

_____

_____

_____

_____

_____

_____

_____

_____

_____

_____

_____

_____

_____

_____

_____

_____

_____

_____

_____

_____

_____

_____

_____

_____

_____

_____

_____

_____

_____

_____

_____

_____

_____

_____

_____

_____

_____

_____

_____

_____

_____

_____

_____

_____

_____

_____

_____

_____

_____

_____

_____

_____

_____

_____

_____

_____

_____

_____

_____

_____

_____

_____

_____

_____

_____

_____

_____

_____

_____

www.ingramcontent.com/pod-product-compliance
Lightning Source LLC
Chambersburg PA
CBHW051044030426
42339CB00006B/182